Rutvik Dharme

SHIVA SAHASTRANAAM STOTRAM ENGLISH

1000 names of Shiva with Meaning in English - Shiva Purana Version

Maha Shiva Book

Instagram : @maha_shiva_

Shiva Sahastranaam Stotram English
1000 names of Shiva with Meaning in English - Shiva
Purana Version

Contents

Introduction

The Shiv Sahastranaam Stotram is the "List of Thousand Names" of Lord Shiva. He is among the main Deities of Hinduism. He is the most glorified God in Hindu Texts that are Vedas, Upanishads, and Puranas. It is Lord Shiva who is present as everything. It is Shiva who is all Gods. In Hindu tradition, Sahastranaam is a type of devotional hymn (Stotram) that lists a thousand names of a Deity. This Devotional Hymn is sung in praise of a Deity.

I am dedicating this book to beloved Lord Shiva who is best among the Gods. Shiva Sahastranaam Stotram is a Devotional Hymn taken from Shiva Puranam. This Devotional Hymn was sung by Lord Vishnu in praise of Lord Shiva. There is a particular story behind this Shiva Sahastranaam, which is mentioned in Shiva Purana. By chanting this Devotional Hymn, Lord Shiva is pleased with his devotee, and completes all his wishes. Chanting this Hymn gives peace, happiness, positiveness, gratefulness, enchanting will, and focus. Shiva Sahasranaam if chanted 3 times daily will remove all your home-related problems within a month. This is a tested fact. Just by reciting the name "Shiva" one becomes free from his sins. Reciting 1000 names of the Lord will give astonishing results.

Chapter 1
Glory of Omkara

Explanation of Pranava from Shiva Purana :
Shiva is in the form of Pranava as mentioned in the Scriptures. One Jyotirlinga is also named Omkareshwara. "Omkareshwara" means he who is the lord of Pranava that is "Om". Om has the capacity to liberate beings in bondage. Living beings are trapped in worldly existence that consists of sorrows as well as some moments of happiness. One who gets elevated from this worldly existence is called Jeevanmukta. He merges back into Shiva.

Shiva is Brahman. He is all-encompassing Lord. Only some people are able to realize his true nature. Such divine souls get liberation. So, the definition of Pranava as stated in Shiva

Purana is that which lifts living beings from Worldly Existence (Prakriti). To attain salvation, one has to cut the ropes of worldly existence. That happens by the grace of Shiva. One has to pass this samsara (worldly existence); its cause is the Great Lord Maheshwara. To win over Maya (illusion of this world), one has to surrender to Shiva. Rudra who is Shiva as glorified in the Vedas is in the form of Pranavam. Shiva is indicated with Om Syllable. It is Shiva who is indicated through Om and Om is the indicator. Bhagwan Shiva himself told this to Bramha and Vishnu. Omkara came from the mouth of Mahadeva. It indicates him only who is the Supreme Godhead. He gave this knowledge to both Bramha and Vishnu. He advised both of them to recite this auspicious mantra. So, they would acquire knowledge about him(Shiva). By reciting the Omkara mantra, the practitioner realizes the true nature of his self. Shiva is the Supreme self of all living entities. Bramha and Vishnu were fighting in arrogance to prove their Supremacy over each other. It was Shiva who destroyed their false ego. It is Lord Sankara who is Supreme actually. On saying of lord Shiva, both the gods Bramha and Vishnu recited Omkara Mantra, and their false pride was destroyed. They realized the Supremacy of Paramashiva. To acquire knowledge of Shiva, one has to recite the Omkara Mantra because he is known through that Pranava also called Taarak Mantra, which means mantra that leads to Liberation. Finally, Knowledge of Shiva leads to Liberation. Shiva Purana states that repetition of Omkara means remembering Supreme Godhead Shiva. Remembrance of God results in the destruction of sins. Taaraka Mantra is identical to Shiva. Shiva is Om. He is five-headed, his five faces are Sadyojata, Vamadeva, Aghora, Ishanaa and Tatpurusha. Sound of Om originated from his five faces. From Northen face, syllable "A" originated. From Western face, syllable "U" originated. From Southern face, syllable "M" originated. From Eastern face, Bindu (Dot) originated. From middle face which is facing in the upward direction, Nada (Sound) originated. All these Syllables, Bindu, and Nada united together to form the syllable, Om. All beings are categorized according to Nama (Name) and Rupa(form). All types of living creatures are pervaded by this Omkara mantra. From Om originated Panchakshari Mantra (five syllabled mantra) "Namah Shivaya". Shiva Purana mentions Pranava and enlists its two types. Pranava mantra is of two Types. One is Sukshma (subtle) and the other one is Sthula (Gross). Omkara is Sukshma and the Panchakshari Mantra "Namah Shivaya" is gross. Both Omkara and Panchakshari are the bestowers of salvation. Shiva blesses those who recite the Pranava mantra. Reciting Pranava increases spiritual power and brings more closer to Shiva.

Chapter 2
Story of Shiv Sahastranaam

Story from Shiva Mahapuran : Once upon a time, the atrocities of the demons started increasing on earth. They became immense and powerful. They started torturing human beings. Demons had enmity with the Gods. They punished Devatas in the heaven and did not allow anyone to worship them.

Dharma started disappearing from the world. The Devatas being saddened by the demons went to Lord Shri Hari Vishnu. All of them informed Lord Vishnu about their grief. After listening to the problems of the Devatas, he assured them that he would do something for their protection. The conduct of demons was unrighteous. Vishnu sent Devatas back to their abodes. He went to Mount Kailash himself and started worshiping Lord Shiva. He established the Linga of Sarveshwara Shiva and started worshipping Lord Shiva with proper process. Shiva is called Sarveshwara because he is the Lord of all. He is Mahadeva because he is the Great God. Srihari did severe penance for Bhagwan Shiva. Yet, Supreme Godhead was not pleased with him. After that, Vishnu started chanting Shiva Sahastranaam to please Shiva. Sahastranaam is a devotional hymn that lists 1000 names sung in the praise of a Deity. Shri Hari would take one name of Shiva and offer one Lotus flower to him. Thus, he spent a lot of time reciting Shiva Sahastranaam. With each name of Supreme Godhead, he used to offer one Lotus. One fine day, Lord Shiva decided to test the Devotion of Vishnu. Lord

Vishnu used to worship him with 1000 lotus flowers every day. Shiva made one flower disappear from the place using his divine powers. When one lotus flower fell short at the time of worship, Vishnu was very surprised and started looking for flower here and there. When the flower was not found anywhere, he offered his eye instead of the flower. Seeing such excellent devotional service of Vishnu, Shiva gave him direct blessings. Lord Shiva was happy with the excellent penance and devotion of Vishnu. After witnessing Lord Shiva, Vishnu started praising him. Then Shiva said "I am pleased with your excellent devotion. What do you want? Please tell me I am ready to grant you various boons." Hearing the words of Shiva, Vishnu said, "O Mahadeva Sarveshwara Shiva you are knower of past, present, and future. You are Antaryamin. You are the one who knows everything. You are the one who gives the desired results to your devotees. O Lord Shiva! At this time, the Demons have created havoc in the entire Universe. All human beings and gods are suffering. . I am not able to control these demons with my weapons, that is why I have come under your refuge. When Shiva heard such words of Vishnu, then he granted him Sudarshan Chakra. Narayana used it and destroyed all the Demons. In this way everyone became happy. Sudarshan Chakra was granted to Vishnu by Lord Shiva. He recited Devotional Hymn which lists 1000 names of Bhagwan Shiva. Shivalinga which was worshipped by Lord Vishnu is called "Harishwara". "Harishwara" means one who is the Lord of Hari (Vishnu). Vishnu offered his Lotus eye to Lord Shiva. This was his excellent Devotion for Lord Shiva. Vishnu is called as "Padmaksha" or "Kamalnayana" because he is Lotus eyed. This was the story of Shiva Sahastranaam that Vishnu recited.

Chapter 3
Benefits of Chanting Shiv Sahastranaam

1)All desires of a Devotee are fulfilled.

2)Whoever recites thousand names of Shiva daily in the morning with pure heart and devotion will get all the siddhis.

3)One becomes free from sorrow and fear.

4)Reciting this great Stotra hundred times definitely brings welfare.

5)All kinds of diseases are destroyed and desired results are obtained.

6)One gets all kinds of happiness and all his wishes are definitely fulfilled.

7)Devotee who recites 1000 names of Shiva attains salvation by getting rid of the hassles of life and death by the grace of Shiva.

8)All sins are destroyed by reading or listening to it.

Note: While reciting, if Om is used before each name of Lord Shiva and putting 'Namah' at the end, then it is extremely beneficial.

Chapter 3
1000 names of Lord Shiva with Meaning

All the names recited by Sri Vishnu along with their meanings. 1000 names of Shiva mentioned in Shiva Purana listed below.

1)Shiva - Highly Auspicious, pure, well-being, peaceful, Supreme consciousness

2)Har - Destroyer of sins committed by Devotees

3)Mrida - Giver of happiness to his Devotees

4)Rudra - Supreme God (Bhagwan) of Vedas, he who makes other cry, Destructive,

Terrible, scary, he who destroys sorrows of the world, one who makes enemies of his devotees suffer, he who is promoted in the form of Veda Dharma (Shiva being essence of Veda Vedanta), he who is in the form of Pranava (OM), he who makes his Devotees realize him, he who enters in humans in the form of Truth.

5)Pushkar - He who is in the form of Sky, he who is non-dual like Sky

6)Pushpalochana - He who has eyes as soft as flower

7)Arthigamya - He who listens to the prayers of his Devotees

8)Sadachar - One with Right Conduct, He who is noble, whose behavior is the Best

9)Sharva - Destroyer of Everything

10)Shambhu - Source of Happiness, he who does welfare of his Devotees

11)Maheshwar - Great God

12)Chandrapid - He who has Crescent moon on his Head

13)Chandramouli - He who uses moon as crown, he who has Crescent moon on his Head

14)Vishwam - He who manifested as

everything, one who is in the form of Worlds

15)Vishwambhareshwar - Maintainer of worlds, Lord of even Vishnu

16)Vedantsaarsandoha - He who has complete knowledge of Vedanta

17)Kapali - He who carries skull in his hands

18)Nilalohita - Red colored one with blue throat, one whose body color is red and he is having blue mark on his neck

19)Dhyanadhar - Base or object of Meditation

20)Aparicchedya - Inexplicable, one who is incapable of being explained

21)Gauribharta - Husband of Gauri

22)Ganeshvara - Lord of Ganas (Ganas are attendants. Attendants of Shiva are called Shivaganas. Shiva is the Lord of those Attendants that's why he is called Ganeshvara.)

23)Ashtamurti - He who has eight Cosmic bodies Sarva, Bhava, Rudra, Ugra, Bheema, Pasupathi, Mahadeva, and Ishana

24)Vishvamurti - All Cosmic Virat Purusha (Bhagwan, Atman, Supreme Godhead), He who is in the form of Entire Universe

25)Trivargswargsadhan - Bestower of Dharma (Righteousness), Artha(Economic

Values), Kama(Pleasure) and Heavenly Worlds

26)Gyangamya - He who is experienced through knowledge

27)Dridhpragya - One with steady intellect

28)Devdev - God of Gods, He who is adorable for Gods, he who is worshipped by Gods

29)Trilochan - Three eyed personality (Shiva is having three eyes. He possesses Surya [Sun], Chandra [Moon] and Agni [Fire] in his three eyes. He burned cupid Kamadeva with his third eye containing fire)

30)Vamdeva - He whose behavior is different from people

31)Mahadev - Great God, God of Gods, he who is worshipped by everyone and who is Lord of everyone

32)Patu - He who is capable of doing everything, Efficient

33)Parivridh - Owner, everyone's Boss, possessor

34)Dridh - He who never gets distracted

35)Vishvaroopa - He who is having Universal form, he who is multiformed

36)Virupaaksh - Odd eyed, one with un-even eyes, three eyed, one with formidable eyes

37)Vagish - Lord of Speech

38)Suchisattam - Best among Holy men, Supreme among Holy men

39)Sarvapramansamvadi - In whom all the proofs and authorities agree that he is Supreme God

40)Vrishank -He who keeps bull as a Sign on his flag

41)Vrishvahan - He who rides on a Bull (Lord Shiva rides on a Bull named Nandi. Bull signifies Dharma(Righteousness). One who is devotee of Shiva and is righteous in his life is dear to Shiva. Therefore, one who follows Dharma is dear to Lord Shiva. Afterall, Shiva is the God of righteousness, who rides on a Bull that signifies Dharma(Righteousness).

42)Ish - Owner, Ruler, God, Controller of all

43)Pinaki - He who has a bow named "Pinaka"

44)Khatvangi - The God who carries knurled club (Khatvanga) weapon [Khatvanga is a weapon or emblem of Shiva]

45)Chitravesh - He whose disguise is very strange

46)Chirantan - Ancient God, Puran Purusha (God,Bramhan,Atman), oldest of all

47)Tamohar - Lord who removes the ego or ignorance, he who removes Tamas(Ignorance) from the life of his devotee

48)Mahayogi - A person who is proficient at Yoga is called as "Yogi". Shiva is the greatest of Yogis. Therefore, he is called "Mahayogi". Yoga originates from Lord Shiva. Knowledge of Yoga was first given by Lord Shiva.

49)Gopta - Protector of all

50)Bramha - He who assumes the form of Bramha for the Creation of Universe, he who creates this Universe

51)Dhurjati - He who is having matted locks

of hair

52)Kalakal - He who is "Time" of Time, he who is Supreme Time, he who is "Death" of even death, he who is beyond the cycle of Time.

53)Krittivasa - He who wears the skin of demon Gajasura as garment

54)Subhag - Blessed, Lucky, fortunate

55)Pranavatmak - He who is denoted in the form of Pranava (Om) [Bhagwan Shiva is Denoted in the form of Omkara. He is Lord of Om(Pranava). Supreme God is denoted with Om]

56)Unnadhra - Free, uplifted, he who does not need anyone's support

57)Purusha - Bhagwan(God), Divine Being, Bramhan, self

58)Jusya - Worthy to be served, worthy of worship

59)Durvasa - He who incarnated as Sage Durvasa

60)Purshasana - Chastiser of Tipuras(Three Cities)

61)Divyayudha - Having Divine weapons like Trishula, Mahapashupata and others

62)Skandguru   -   Father   of   Kartikeya, preceptor of Skanda (Kartikeya)

63)Parameshthi - He who stays at the acme

64)Paratpara - Cause of all causes , Ultimate cause of everything, Greater than the Greatest

65)Anadimadhyanidhan   -   One   with   no beginning, middle or end (Shiva is Unborn. He is Ultimate cause of this Universe. He was there in the past. He is in the present and he will be there in the future. He is deathless)

66)Girish - Lord of Mountains, Lord of Kailash Mountain

67)Girijadhav - Husband of Girija(Parvati)

68)Kuberbandhu - He who considers Kubera as his Friend (Kubera is God of Wealth. He is the friend of Lord Shiva. Kubera got wealth by the grace of Shiva)

69)Srikantha - He who is having Glorious Neck

70)Lokvarnottam - Best among the groups of people, varnas, castes in the world

71)Mridu - Soft, one with gentle nature, he who is soft-hearted

72)Samadhivedya - He who can be realized through Trance or the highest state of Meditation

73)Kodandi - Archer, he who is holding a bow

74)Nilakantha - Blue throated one, blue necked (Lord Shiva's neck turned blue when he consumed Halaahala poison for the sake of world. Therefore, he is called Nilakantha)

75)Parashadhi - He who is having Parashu (Axe), he who uses Axe as a weapon

76)Vishalaksha - Big eyed

77)Mrigvyadha - Hunter of Animals (Shiva took the form of Kiratha to test Arjuna, Shiva disguised himself as Hunter)

78)Suresh - Lord of Gods

79)Suryatapan - Scorcher of the Sun, he who gave punishment to Sun God

80)Dharmadham - Lord of Dharma(Righteousness), presiding deity of Virtue and Righteousness

81)Shamashetra - He who forgives his Devotee, field of forgiveness

82)Bhagwan - Supreme Personality of Godhead, Supreme Godhead, Bramhan, Atman, Purusha, he who is full in six opulences, who has full strength, fame, wealth, knowledge, beauty and renunciation

83)Bhagnetrabhita - Splitter of the eyes of Bhaga, he who blinded Bhaga in the form of

Veerabhadra. (Sometimes because of Kalpabheda same story differs and Shiva himself comes to destroy Daksha Yagya. He himself pulls out the eyes of Bhaga)

84)Ugra - Fierce, he who takes Terrible and fierce form at the time of Destruction

85)Pashupati - Lord of Pashus, Lord of Animals, Lord of souls who are trapped in the cycle of birth and death, giver of Liberation to beings in Bondage

86)Tarsya - He who is in the form of Garudra (Eagle), Identical with Garuda

87)Priyabhakta - He who loves his Devotees, he who is favourite of his devotees

88)Parantapa - He who destroys his Enemies, scorcher of Enemies, slayer of his Enemies, he who makes his Enemy cry

89)Data - Giver (Shiva gives every time, he never takes. People in this world are suffering, they blame God. They are completely wrong. They are suffering due to their own Karma (actions). Shiva does not interfere in Karma. One who is Righteous, Shiva definitely supports him because Shiva is God of Righteousness)

90)Dayakar - Compassionate

91)Daksh - Skillful, capable of doing everything

92)Kapardi/Kapardin - He who is having matted locks of hair, matted haired personality

93)Kamshasan - He who rules over Cupid Kamadeva, Chastiser of Cupid, He who burnt Cupid Kamadeva into ashes, he who is unaffected by Lust and passion

94)Smashananilaya - He who resides in Cremation Ground

95)Shukshma सूक्ष्म - Subtle

96)Smashanastha - He who stays in Cremation Ground

97)Maheshwar - Great God, God of Gods,

Maha Ishwara

98)Lokakarta - He who is Creator of this World

99)Mrigapati - Lord of Deer, he who holds deer in his left upper hand.

100)Mahakarta - Creator of Everything, Great Maker

101)Mahaushadhi - Great Medicine

102)Uttar - Giver of Liberation from repeated cycles of Birth and Death

103)Gopti - Lord of heaven, earth, animals, speech, rays, senses and water

104)Gopta - Protector

105)Gyangamya - He who is attained through perfect Knowledge

106)Puratan - Most Ancient God (Shiva is the most Ancient God)

107)Niti - Justice

108)Suniti - Good Justice and policy

109)Suddhatma - Pure Soul, Holy Spirit, Super Soul

110)Soma - He who is accompanied with his Consort Uma(Soma means Shiva + Uma. Soma is Shiva. When Shiva is depicted with his wife Uma and his son Skanda (Kartikeya) that Murthy is called as Somaskanda Murthy)

111)Somrat - He who showers his blessings on Chandra (Moon God). Here, Soma means Moon

112)Sukhi - He who is always happy and filled with joy

113)Somap - Somap means he who drinks Soma juice (Soma juice is a Divine Drink which is offered to Shiva. Shiva is also called as "Soma" because he is presiding Deity of Soma Plant from which Soma juice is extracted). Somap also means preserver and protector of Chandra (Moon God). "Soma" is the word which is also used for Moon God.

114)Amritapa - He who drinks Nectar of Immortality through trance or highly meditative state

115)Saumya - Gentle, one who is soft for his Devotees

116)Mahateja - Filled with Great Splendour

117)Mahadyuti - One with Great Splendour and Brilliance

118)Tejomaya - He who is full of Lustre, shining

119)Amritmaya - He who is full of Nectar

120)Annamaya - He who is in the form of

Food

121)Sudhapati - He who is Lord of Amrita (Nectar)

122)Ajatashatru - He who never considers others as his Enemy, he who never develops feeling of Enemity for others

123)Aalok - He who is in the form of Light

124)Sambhavya - Honorable and Respectable

125)Havyavahan - He who is in the form of Agni(Fire), he who is carrier of sacrificial offerings i.e Agni (Fire), one who is Agni Swaroopa [Shiva himself is in the form of Agni(Fire)]

126)Lokakar - Maker of Worlds

127)Vedkar - Creator of Vedas, Origin of Vedas, from whom Vedas originate

128)Sutrakaar - He who created Maheshwara Sutras by playing his Damru (Musical Instrument in the hand of Shiva) [When Shiva played his Damru, from the sound of that Damru originated Maheshwar Sutras, Sanskrit Alphabets originate from Maheshwar Sutras], Therefore, Shiva is called as Sutrakaar

129)Sanatan - Eternal

130)Kapilacharya - Founder of Samkhya school of Hindu Philosophy

131)Vishvadipti - Light of Universe , one who lights up everyone with his splendour

132)Trilochan - Three-eyed God

133)Pinakpani - He who is holding Pinaka bow in his hands

134)Bhudev - God of Earth viz; Mahadeva

135)Svastida - He who does the welfare of all, bestower of Well-being, bestower of wealth

136)Svastikrita - Bestower of well-being

137)Sudhi - Intelligent

138)Dhatrudhama - He who feeds world with

his own powers

139)Dhamakara - Creator of Lustre

140)Sarvag - All-pervasive, all-pervading being

141)Sarvagochar - He who is present in all, he who is visible to all

142)Bramhasrk - Creator of Bramha (One among Tridevas viz; Bramha, Vishnu, Rudra)

143)Vishvasrk - Creator of the Universe

144)Sarga - He who is in the form of Entire

Creation, one who is in the form of entire Cosmos

145)Karnikarpriya - He who is fond of Oleander Flowers (Kaner Flower/कनेर पुष्प)

146)Kavi - Poet

147)Shakha - In the appearance of of Rishi named Shakha

148)Vishakh - Rishi named Vishakh, in the Form of Kartikeya

149)Goshakh - He who propagates various branches of Vedas

150)Shiva - Highly Auspicious, pure, well-being, peaceful, Supreme Conciousness

151)Bhishakanuttama - Excellent Physician, best among physicians, He is in the Form of Dhamvantari or Physician providing well-being to all

152)Gangaplavodak - River Ganga flows in his matted Locks of hair. Therefore, he is called Gangaplavodak

153)Bhavya - Fully propitious, good

154)Pushkal - Abundant, eminent one, complete or pervasive

155)Sthapati - Architect of all the Worlds

156)Sthira - Stable and steady

157)Vijitatma - Self-conqueror , one who has control over his senses, a triumphant super soul

158)Vidheyatma - Self-controlled, excellent soul of submissive worlds, controller of body, mind and senses according to his own will

159)Bhutavahansarathi - Controller of body made up of Panchabhootas(Five Elements) in the form of Mind

160)Sagan - Accompanied by Ganas(Attendants), he who has Pramatha Ganas with him always

161)Ganakaya - He who is in the form of Gana(his own Attendant), he who is with Ganas as a guard, Indestructible along with Pramathaganas

162)Sukirti - One with good fame, highly reputed

163)Chinnasanshaya - He whose doubts are destroyed, he who destroys doubts of his Devotees

164)Kamadeva - Identical with Cupid, Lord of Desires, he who is in the form of Cupid Kamadeva

165)Kamapala - Bestower of Fulfillments, he who completes wishes of his devotees, protector of Desires

166)Bhasmoddhuulitha Vigrah - He who applies ashes all over his body, whose body is dusted with Holy Ashes(Bhasma, Vibhooti)

167)Bhasmapriya - He who is fond of sacred Ashes, an enthusiastic of sacred Ash(Bhasma, Vibhooti)

168)Bhasmashayi - He who is fond of laying in sacred Ashes (Bhasma)

169)Kami - Endower of Desires, Lover of his Devotees

170)Kantha - Highly Attractive

171)Kritagama - Creator of Agamas, executor of Vedas/Agamas

172)Samavarta - He who whirls the wheel of Worldly Existence, Executor of Life Cycles

173)Anivrttatma - He whose soul never turns back, he whose soul is not movable [Anivrttatma" which means he whose soul is not movable which again means because he is present everywhere, everything exists in him, for him there is no place outside to pervade further. Therefore, he is not movable and fixed on one place.]

174)Dharmapunja - Mass of Virtues, consummated Virtue

175)Sadashiva - Auspicious forever, always propitious

176)Akalmasha - Devoid of Sins, Sinless

177)Chaturbahu - Four armed

178)Duravasa - He who is difficult to access, he who is difficult to bear in hearts even for Yogis, Attainable with rigorous Tapasya or Commitment

179)Durasada - Un-conquerable, whom none may overcome, only conquered through Devotion

180)Durlabha - Very rare, achieved only with highest devotion

181)Durgam - He who is witnessed with enormous difficulty, difficult of being attained

182)Durg - He who protects his Devotees from sins

183)Sarva ayudha Visharada - Expert in wielding weapons, Versatile in the art of weaponry like Sastra

184)Adhyatmya Yognilaya - Expert in Yoga Practice to destroy miseries of body and mind, expert in Spiritual practices

185)Sutantu - He who wears Universe as his clothes, he who keeps with him the wide World

186)Tantuvardhana - He who broadens the worlds

187)Shubhang - Having auspicious limbs, he who is having beautiful body parts

188)Lokasarang - Essence of the Worlds

189)Jagdish - Lord of Universe, Controller of Universe

190)Janardana - He who demolishes sorrows of Human Beings, works to fulfill prayers of his Devotees

191)Bhasmashuddhikara - He who purifies with sacred Ashes, causing purity with sacred Ashes (Bhasma, Vibhooti)

192)Meru - He who stays at Meru Mountain, he who is centre of attraction like Meru Mountain

193)Ojasvi - Vigorous

194)Suddhavigrah - He who has pure body, pure physique

195)Asadhya - Unachievable, he who is not easy to realise[Shiva is Unachievable for those who are devoid of Bhakti or Devotion)

196)Sadhusadhya - Achievable easily by saintly person, possible of realisation only by virtuous

197)Bhrtyamarkatroopdhrk - He who

assumes the form of Hanuman

198)Hiranyareta - He who is in the form of Agni(Fire) or Gold Semened

199)Pauran - He who is Glorified in all Puranas as Supreme Godhead, Ancient one [Shiva is also called as Pauran Purusha]

200)Ripujeevhar - Destroyer of Enemies, Slayer of Enemies

201)Bali - Powerful, Strong, Enjoyer of Supreme Strength

202)Mahahrada - Ocean full of Eternal Happiness

203)Mahagart - He who is in the form of Great Sky, Lord of Great Illusions

204)Siddha Vrindara Vanditah - Saluted by Siddhas and Devas, saluted by Gods

205)Vyaghracharmambar - He who wears skin of Tiger

206)Vyali - He who wears poisonous snakes as his ornament

207)Mahabhuta - Virat Purusha, Supreme Being who is unaffected by three modes of time which are past, present and future

208)Mahanidhi - Great Storehouse

209)Amritash - Eternal enjoyer of Nectar

210)Amritavapu - He who has indestructible physique, Indestructible Being

211)Panchajanya - Shiva as Agni in Five Forms as manifested in Yajnas, favourable to the five classes of Beings, Counch shell named Panchajanya

212)Prabhanjana - Shiva as 'Vayu' surrounded by Illusions among mortals, He who is in the form of "Vayu", Hailstorm, Destructive

213)Panchavimsati Tatvasthah - Shiva as Twenty five Tatvas viz. Pancha Bhutas, Pancha Tanmatras, Pancha Karmendriyas,

Pancha Jnanendrias and Pancha Anthakaranas

214)Parijata - Fulfiller of desires of devotees, celestial tree

215)Paratpara - Greater than the Greatest

216)Sulabha - Easy to please with sincerity and devotion, easily accessible to righteous people

217)Suvrata - He who performs Vratha type of penance to encourage others, He who guides devotees to perform simple and easy Vrathas

218)Sura - Champion, Heroic

219)Bramhavedanidhi - Shiva as the Source of Bramha and Vedas

220)Nidhi - Creator of Universe

221)Varnashram Guru - Master of Four Varnas of Brahmana, Vaishya, Kshatriya and Sudras as also Four Ashramas viz. Brahmacharya, Garhasthya, Vanaprastha and Sanyasa

222)Varni - Celibate, Shiva as Brahmachari or Vidyarthi (student)

223)Shatrujit - Conquerer of Enemies

224)Shatrutapana - Scorcher of Enemies

225)Aashram - Provider of peace, Provider of respite to those engaged in the worldly affairs

226)Kshaman - Destoyer of suffering caused by repeated cycles of Birth and Death

227)Kshama - Terminator at the End

228)Jnanavan - He who is full of Knowledge, Knowledgeable, wise

229)Achaleshwar - Lord of Mountains, Chief of Stable beings like Earth and Mountains

230)Pramanbhuta - Authoritative proof

231)Durjey - Difficult to be known

232)Suparn - Like a Tree with branches as Vedas, Like a eagle with feathers as Vedas

233)Vayuvahan - He who makes airflow to move with his Terror

234)Dhanurdhar - Archer, Processor of Bow named Pinaka

235)Dhanurveda - Knower of Dhanurveda, The Originator of the Science of Bow and Arrows

236)Gunarashi - Totality of Gunas or Qualities like, Vidya, Kriya, Satya, Daya, Ahimsa, Shanti, Dama, Dhyeya, Dhyana, Dhriti, Medha, Niti, Kanthi, Drishti, Lajja, Pushti, Prathishtha and so on, he who is filled with all good Qualities

237)Gunakara - Storehouse of Qualities

238)Satya - Truth, Embodiment of Truth

239)Satyapar - Practioner of Truth

240)Adin - Non-distressed

241)Dharmang - Dharma's various Limbs like Feet as Vedas, Handslike Varaha Murthi, Brahma like Face, Agni like Tongue, Hairs like Kusha Grass, Eyes like Day and Night, Ornaments like Vedanth & Srithis, Soma like Blood, and so on

242)Dharma Sadhana - He who is practice of

Dharma (Shiva is God of Righteousness)

243)AnanthaDrishthi - He who has Infinte Vision

244)Anand - Blissful, Eternal Bliss, Happiness

245)Dand - He who punishes the wicked, he who is in the form of punishment

246)Damayita - Suppressor, Scorcher of Demons, he who punishes the wicked

247)Dama - Controller of Devas, Beings, and Tatvas like Maha Bhutas, Indriyas, Tanmatras and so on

248)Abhivadya - Worthy of Worship, worthy

of being praised, worthy of being saluted

249)Mahamaya - He who is Illusion maker, he who is unaffected by illusion, he who can delude even Illusion

250)Vishvakarma Visharada - He who has capacity to create Entire Universe

251)Vitraga - Complete Celibate, devoid of passion, destroyer of Desires and Hatred

252)Vinitatma - He who softens the personality of His devotees

253)Tapasvi - Ascetic

254)Bhuta Bhavanah - He provides mental

development of His Devotees, Creator of all living beings

255)Unmattavesha - One with strange disguise

256)Pracchanna - Hidden one

257)Jitakam - Conquerer of Lust

258)Ajitpriya - Affectionate to Lord Vishnu

259)Kalyana Prakrithi - Gracious featured, he who has good nature, Compassionate God

260)Kalp - He who is capable of doing everything, root cause of Entire Creation

261)Sarvalokaprajapati - Sovereign of All Worlds, Creator of all worlds

262)Tarasvi - Forceful, fastest

263)Taraka - Liberator, he who let his devotees cross the rough oceans of 'Samsara' or repeated cycles of Birth and Death

264)Dhiman - Intelligent

265)Pradhan - Chief

266)Prabhu - Protector

267)Avyaya - Imperishable

268)Lokapala - Protector of the worlds

269)Antarhitatma - Hideout of His Real Self due to Illusion

270)Kalpadi - The very beginning of Kalpa

271)Kamlekshan - Lotus-eyed

272)Veda Shasteartha Tatvagya - Knower of principles and meanings of Vedas, Best Comprehender of Tatva Jnana of Vedas and Shastras

273)Aniyam - He is Knowledge by Himself and excels in imparting it to others, he who has no restrictions

274)Niyamashraya - Supporter of Everyone

275)Chandra - He who is in the form of Moon

276)Surya - He who is in the form of Sun, Shiva as the origin of Surya.

277)Shani - He who is in the form of Shani(Saturn)

278)Ketu - Planet Ketu

279)Varanga - Having perfect shaped limbs

280)Vidrumachhavi - He who has red-complexion, he whose body colour is red

281)Bhaktivashya - He who is in the control of Devotees, subservient to Devotion

282)Parabrahman - Great Bramhan, Bhagwan, Atman, Purusha, Supreme God

283)Mrigabanapurna - He who discharged arrows on deer in the form of Hunter, He who searches his devotees like arrow searching deers

284)Anagh - Devoid of Sins, faultless

285)Adri - He who is in the form of Mountains

286)Adralay - He who resides in Mountains, resident of Kailash Mountain

287)Kanth - Luminous, everyone's favourite

288)Paramatma - Super Soul

289)Jagadguru - Universal Teacher

290)Sarva Karmalaya - Target God for daily devotional activities of common people

291)Tusht - Always Happy, Highly self-contented

292)Mangalya - Auspicious for His devotees

293)Mangalakritah - He who is filled with auspicious powers

294)Maha Tapah - He who performs the Greatest Meditation to Create the Mega Universe

295)Dirgha Tapah – He who executes longtime meditation for Sustenance of Universe

296)Sthavishtha - Greatest, very strong, largest

297)Sthavirah Dhruvah - Most Ancient and Stable

298)Ahah Samvatsarah - He who is in the form of day and year as Time

299)Vyapti - All pervasive

300)Pramana - Proof

301)Param Tapah - Supreme Penance

302)Samvatsarakara - Player of cyclical movement of years

303)Mantra Pratyay - He who transcends Himself through recitals of Veda Mantras

304)Sarva Darshan - He who reveals the whole world as real

305)Aja - Unborn

306)Sarveshwara - Lord of all, God of all

307)Siddha - Support of Sages

308)Mahareta - Super Virile

309)Mahabala - Super Strong, He who has

Great Strength

310)Yogi Yogya - Ideally deserving Yoga practitioner

311)Mahateja - With great Radiance, Lustrous

312)Siddhi - Achievement

313)Sarvadi - He who is beginning of all, Creator of all, origin of everything

314)Agrah - He who never accept the sinful

315)Vasu - He who keeps all living beings within him

316)Vasumana - Kind Hearted, Merciful, he who is unaffected by preferences of liking or hatred

317)Satya - Truth, he who is in the form of Truth

318)Sarvapaapaharo Har - Destroyer of Sins, Remover of Sins

319)Sukirtishobhana - He who is highly reputed and famous

320)Sriman - He who is allied with his wife Uma

321)Vedang - His hands are like branches of Vedas therefore, he is called as "Vedang" (He constitutes the branches of Vedas)

322)Vedavinmunih - The Sage who is an adept in Vedas, knower of Vedas

323)Bhrajishnu - Shining and Radiant

324)Bhojana - Food

325)Bhokta - Enjoyer, he who enjoys the food

326)Lokanath - Lord of Universe

327)Duradhar - He who is difficult to attain by unrighteous people, Unconquerable

328)Amrita Shashvat - Undecaying and

Everlasting

329)Shantah - Peaceful

330)Banhasta Pratapvaan - Brave Archer, Valorous Archer holding now in his hand

331)Kamandalu Dhara - He who carries Kamandalu or a Holy vessel in his hand, he who is holding water pot

332)Dhanvi - He who carries bow named Pinaka in his hands

333)Avanmanasa Gocharah - Impossible to comprehend by Physical or mental faculties

334)Atindriyah Mahamaya - He who is far

beyond the reach of Physical or Mental features and he who is the Great Illusion

335)Sarvavasa - He who is abode of Everyone

336)Chatushpathah - He who prompts to four paths to his Devotees, giver of Dharma (Righteousness) , Artha (Economic Values), Kama (Pleasure) , Moksha (Liberation) to his Devotees

337)Kalayogi - He who cautions devotees about the end of their lives, He who is united in Time

338)Mahanaad - Loud Sound, Great Sound

339)Mahotsaho Mahabala - He who is filled

with Great Enthusiasm and Strength

340)Maha Buddhi - Highly Intelligent, Great Intellect

341)Maha Virya - The Unique Producer of the Worlds, Extremely Valorous

342)Bhutachari - He whose company consists of Extra Territorial Beings like Goblins

343)Purandar - Slayer of Tripurasur

344)Nishachara - Active Trekker at Night

345)Pretachari - He who moves along with Groups of Ghosts and Goblins

346)Mahashakti Mahadhyuti - He who is extremely powerful and He who has unrivalled luminosity

347)Anirdesya Vapu - He possesses an outstanding Physique

348)Shriman - Prosperous, Wealthy, he who has glow of Prosperity

349)Sarvacharya Manogati - He guides Various Teachers in imparting Knowledge

350)Bahu Shrutah - Origin of several Holy Scriptures

351)Maha Maya - He who is Inventor of the Great Illusion, Illusion maker, unaffected personality by illusion

352)Niyatatma - He who has control over his desires

353)Dhruvadhruv - Eternal and non-eternal, Steady and Unsteady

354)Ojas Tejo Dyuti Dharah - He carries Life, Might, Light and such other fantastic features

355)Janak - Creator of Everyone, Father

356)Sarvashasan - Ruler of Everyone, Lord of Everyone, Chastiser of all

357)Nrityapriya - He who is fond of dance

358)Nityanritya - He who does Tandava dance daily, He who is eternally doing cosmic Tandava dance

359)Prakashatma - Luminous Soul, Epitome of Brilliance

360)Prakashak - Illuminator, He who distributes Illumination

361)Spashtakshar - Distinct Word like OM, He who is denoted by Pranava "OM"

362)Budha - Intelligent, Wise, Full of Knowledge

363)Mantra - He who is in the form of Mantras of Four Vedas viz; Rigved,

Yajurveda, Samveda, Atharvaveda

364)Samanah - Impartial

365)Sara Samplavah - He who is like a boat which helps to cross ocean of birth and death, He who is Liberator from repeated cycles of Birth and Death

366) Yugadi Krithyugavartha - He who rotates the Yugas

367)Gambhir - Serious and Complex due to knowledge and experience

368)Vrisha Vahana - Bull Vehicled, He who rides on a Bull

369)Ishta - Worshipped by everyone owing to his Supremecy, the most sought after

370)(a)Avishishtha - Devoid of Attributes (b)Vishishtha - Most Distinguished

371)Sistesta - God of Polite People

372)Sulabha - Easily attainable by pure Devotees , Easy of access

373)Saarshodhan - Purifier of Essence

374)Tirtharoop - Holy Place, He who is in the form of Holy Centre

375)Tirthanama - He who has the various names of Holy places, his name is holy and pure by uttering his name itself Devotee will get liberated from repeated cycles of Birth and Death therefore Shiva is Tirthanama

376)Thirtha drishya - He who blesses or enables of viewing various Thirthas like Kashi

377)Tirthada - Bestower of Tirthas

378)Apaanidhi - He who is in the form of Oceans

379)Adhishtana - He is the King or support of the Srishti/Creation

380)Durjey - Difficult of Access

381)Jayakalavita - Knower of the time of

Conquest

382)Pratishthitha - Well-known, well established, His magnitude and might are well established

383)Pramanajna - He has the full awareness of Pramanas or Proofs both direct or subtle

384)Hiranyakavach - He who wears Golden shield

385)Hari - Shri Hari Vishnu, He who is in the form of Vishnu

386)Vimochan - He who liberates his devotee from repeated cycles of Birth and Death, He is the reliever of the three kinds of Tapatrayas or tribulations viz. of Adi bhautika, Adhyatmika and Adi Daivika nature

387)Suragana - He assumes the traits and strengths of all the Devas

388)Vidyeshah - He is the root of all 'Vidyas' and also the bestower of the deserved ones, Source of knowledge

389)Bindu Samsrayah - Pranava or Omkara is his own manifestation, He who manifested into Pranava Om

390)Balroop - He who is in the form of child

391)Aabalonunmattah - Devoid of False pride of his powers

392)Avikarta - Devoid of faults

393)Gahan - The Unknowable; none could comprehend the Lord's ways of thought or action

394)Guha - He who is hidden behind the worldly illusion

395)Karana - Source of Creation

396)Kaarana - Cause of Creation

397)Karta - The Doer, Creator

398)Sarvabandhavimochana - The Liberator of all hindrances

399)Vyavasaya - Determined to be in Sat-Chit-Ananda Position (Full of Spiritual Knowledge)

400)Vyavasthana - He who sets up the 'Varnashrama' format

401)Sthanada - Decides individual positions and duties

402)Jagdadijah - He who exists at be very beginning of the Universe, he who was present before Hiranyagarbha Golden Cosmic Egg

403)Guruda - Provider of weighty things, Bestower of the things which are best for his Devotees

404)Lalit - Beautiful, attractive and soft personality

405)Abheda - Non-dual manifestor, he who alone exist in the form of different Gods, he who is non-different from entire existence

406)Bhavatatmani Samsthitha - He exists as the Innermost Soul of the bodies made by Pancha Bhutas or Five Elements, he who is stationed in soul

407)Vireswara - Lord of the Valiant, Lord of Heroes

408)Veerbhadra - He who manifested himself into Veerbhadra (Eternal Shiva Gana destroyer of Daksha's sacrifice)

409)Virasanvidhi - Master of Valiant's posture, he who sits in Valiant's posture

410)Virat - Universal formed

411)Virachudamani - Crest jewel among Heroes, Best of all Valiant personalities

412)Vetta - Intelligent, full of Knowledgeable personality, knower

413)Chidananda - Happy always, full with eternal bliss

414)Nadidhaar - He who is holding Ganga river in his matted hairs

415)Agyadhar - Holder of behests

416)Trishuli - He who uses Trishula (Trident) as his weapon, holding the Trident in his hands

417)Shipivishta - Radiant, Lustrous, surrounded by bright rays, stationed in rays,Vishnu, in Yajnas he manifests Himself as Lord Vishnu

418)Shivalaya - He resides at all Places that are propitious, he who is in the form of Shivalaya (Shiva Temple)

419)Valakhilya - Rishi Valakhilya

420)Mahachaapa - Great Archer

421)Tigmanshu - Shiva as Sun God

422)Badhirah - Chooses to be hard of hearing sometimes

423)Khag - Traversing the Sky

424)Abhiram - Most Beautiful, resting place of Yogis

425)Susharana - Provider of security and refuge

426)Subrahmanya - Ideal Explainer of Vedic knowledge and its interpreters, care taker of Bramhanas, Identical with Kumara

427)Sudhapati - Lord of Nectar

428)Maghavan Kaushikah - Shiva as Indra

429)Goman - As the Chief of Cows and cowherds, full of bright rays, stationed in Bright rays

430)Viram - Ultimate Stoppage, Final destination of all

431)Sarvasadhan - He who is having all equipments

432)Lalataksha - He who is having Third Eye on his Forehead

433)Vishvadeha - Universal-bodied, entire Universe is his body

434)Saar - Essence, he who exist at the time of annihilation of the Universe

435)Samsarachakra Bhrit - The Holder of the Cycle of Life

436)Amogha Danda - Giver of irretrievable punishment, his punishment never goes futile that's why he is called as Amogh Dand

437)Madhyastha - Neutral

438)Hiranya - Golden, Radiant, Epitome of Radiance

439)Brahma Varchasi - He who is having Bramhanical Lustre

440)Paramartha - He who grants Salvation, Greatest Entity

441)Paromayi - Wielder of Maya (Great Illusion), He who is the origin of Outstanding Maya

442)Shambharah - He who awards propitiousness

443)Vyaghra Lochanah - He who has the frightening look of a Tiger

444)Ruci - Bright , Brightness, Interest

445)Virinchi - He who is in the form of Brahman (Upanishads glorify that Bhagwan Shiva as Bramhan Ultimate Supreme Reality)

446)Svarbandhu - He who is like brother for Devas(Gods) in Heaven

447)Vachaspati - Lord of Speech

448)Aharpati - Lord of Day, he who is in the form of Surya Sun God, the Sun

449)Ravih - Shiva as the distributor of Nava Rasas on nine Emotions drawn from the Sun - viz. Karuna or Kindness, Bhayanak or Fright, Krodha or anger, Shringara or Attractiveness, Hasya or Comedy, Raudra or Fury, Vira or heroism, Bhibhatsa or disgust and Shanta or Peace

450)Virochanah - Shiva as Agni or Fire, Sun, moon or fire, distributer of light in different ways

451)Skand - God Kartikeya

452)(a)Shastha - He who orders or is the Maker of Rules (b)Vaivaswato - Sage Vaivaswa (c)Yama - Yama the Son of Sun and the God of Death

453)Yukthirunnathi Kirthi - Nyayamurthi, the Famed Ashtanga Yogi Shiva

454)Sanuragah - Affectionate to Devotees, he who loves his Devotees

455)Paranjaya - Always Victorious, he who wins over others in the battlefield

456)Kailasapathi - Lord of Kailasa Mountain

457)Kanth - Attractive, Bright and Radiant

458)Savita - Creator of all Beings, Creator of Universe

459)Ravi Lochana - He who is having Sun like eyes

460)(a)Vidvottam - Best among Knowledgeable personalities (b)Vishvottam - Excellent in the Universe

461)Veetbhaya - Devoid of any Fright

462)Vishwabharta - Supporter of the Universe

463)Anivarith - Unstoppable

464)Nitya - Timeless irrespective of the

Beginning or End of the Universe, Eternal

465)Nitya Kalyan - Always Auspicious, he who does invariable welfare

466)PunyaSravana Kirthana - He whose devotional Hymns are always auspicious and meritorious

467)Durashrava - He who is able to hear from long distance because he(Shiva) is all pervasive means present everywhere

468)Vishvasaha - Forbearer of Everything

469)Dheyah - Final destination, Worthy of Meditation, Worthy of being meditated upon

470)Duswapna Nashan - Destroyer of bad dreams

471)Uttaranah - Who could safely ship through the Ocean of Worldly life, Giver of Liberation from repeated cycles of Birth and Death

472)Dushkritiha - Destroyer of Sins, destroyer of wicked deeds

473)Vijneya - Worthy of being known

474)Dussaha - Unbearable

475)Abhava - Unborn, eternal, he who is beyond cycles of Birth and Death

476)Anadi - Eternal, he who has no beginning

477)Bhurbhuva Lakshmi - He who is centre of attraction in Bhur Bhuva lokas Wealth and Glory of Earth

478)Kiriti - He who is wearing the crown

479)Tridashadhipa - He as the Chief of Devas

480)Vishvagopta - Protector of World

481)Vishvakarta - Creator of World

482)Suvir - Good Hero

483)Ruchirangadah - Gorgeously limbed

484)Janana - He who creates all the Beings

485)Jana janmadih - The essential cause of Creation

486)Pritiman - The Affectionate

487)Nitiman - Ethical

488)Dhava - Lord of Everyone

489)Vasishtha - He who has control over his senses, Sage Vasishtha

490)Kashyap - Sage Kashyap

491)Bhanu - Dazzling or he who is in the form of Sun

492)Bhim - He who is frightening for his Opponents, Terrible

493)Bhima Parakramah - He who is a Demolisher of Asuras (Demons), he who exploits terribly his opponents

494)Pranava - Omkara , the mystic syllable Om

495)Satdyatacharah - Observer of Truthfulness and Virtuosity

496)Mahakosh - Great Treasure

497)Mahadhan - He who has great Prosperity

498)Janmadhip - Lord of Birth

499)Mahadev - Great God

500)Sakalagamaparag - He who has mastered Vedas

501)Tatvam -Tat or That, Am-you, Asi-are is the literal meanings; or Aham-I , Brahma-The Super Soul, Asmi-am; or Deepseated in Brahma's position

502)Tatvavit - He who realizes the Essence of Tatva

503)Ekatma - The Supreme Soul is unique

504)Vibhu - All pervasive, all pervading

505)Vishvabhushan - The Ornament of the

World

506)Rishi - Sage, The Knower of the Unknown; 'Vishvadhipo Rudro Maharshih' is Veda

507)Bramhanah - Knower of Bramhan

508)Aishwaryajanmajaratigah - He who is beyond wealth, prosperity, birth and death

509)Pancha Yagna samutpatthih - Generator of Five kinds of Yagnas on daily basis viz. Deva Yagna or worship to family deity; Brahma Yagna or Practice of Vedas and other Sciptures; Pitri Yagnas to enhance family values; Bhuta Yagna or the spirit of caring and sharing with others including animals and birds; and Nara Yagna providing hospitality to colleagues, neighbours, friends or any body else

510)Vishvesh - Lord of Universe

511)Vimalodaya - He who is Maker of all movable and immovable objects

512)Atmayoni - He who is having self as a source

513)Anadyantha - He has no beginning nor end

514)Vatsalah - Affectionate

515)Bhaktaloka dhrit - The bearer of the

Devotees

516)Gayatrivallabh - He who is lover of Gayatri Mantra

517)Pranshuh - Double brightened by Sunrays

518)Vishvavasa - Abode of the Universe

519)Prabhakar - He who is in the form of Sun God, Shiva as the most prominent form of early morning Sun

520)Shishu - Infant

521)Girirat - He who likes to stay at Kailash Mountain

522)Samrat - Highest Emperor

523)(a)Sushenah - He who is having a huge army of 'Ganas' (b)Surashatru - Deva's Enemy

524)Amogha Arishtanemi - Sinless and Provider of boons to the Virtuous

525)Kumud - He who lightens the burden of Earth by removing the undesirable

526)Vigatajvara - He who is devoid of various kinds of physical ailments

527)Svayamjyotirstanurjyothi - Self illuminated subtle luminosity

528)Atmajyoti - Ever Radiant Soul

529)Achanchala - Steady and Stable

530)Pingala - Tawny Coloured, Golden Coloured

531)Kapilasmashruh - He who has the moustache and beard of golden colour

532)Bhalanetra - He who is having Third eye on his forehead

533)Thrayi thanuh - All the Vedas and Worlds are his forms

534)Jnana Skandhah Maha Niti - Giver of a Storage of Jnana to His devotees to enable them to achieve salvation

535)Vishvotpatti - Creator of Worlds, Lord of Universe

536)Upaplava - Destroyer

537)Bhago Vivasvan aditya - Shiva in the three forms of Bhagah, Visasvah and Aditya

538)Yogaparah - He who is Great Guide to Yogis

539)Divaspathi - The Chief of Heavens, Owner of Heavenly Abodes

540)Kalyana Guna namah - He has the names of auspiciousness

541)Paapaha - Destroyer of Sins, demolisher of the sins of devotees

542)Punya Darshanah - Vision of Virtue's personification, of meritorious Vision

543)Udara kirthih - Esteemed personality, of liberal renown

544)Udyogi - Highly industrious in the context of Creating the Universe

545)Sadyogi - Best Yogi , Supreme Meditator

546)Sadasanmaya - He who is Always engaged in looking after the welfare of everybody

547)Nakshatramali - He who is in the form of Sky, decorated with the garlands of stars

548)Nakesh - Lord of Heavens

549)Swadhishtana Shadasraya - Shiva who is at the Seat of Vital Force

550)Pavitra Paaphari - Always Auspicious, Pure, Sinless, holy, Destroyer of Sins

551)Manipur - Fulfiller of desires including gains of riches including jewellery, He who is in the form of Manipur Chakra

552)Nabhogati - He who freely moves around the skies

553)Hrithpundarikamaseenah - He who resides in Heart, Comfortably Seated on the lotus like hearts of Yogis

554)Shakra - He who is in the form of Indra, Identical with Indra

555)Shanta - Peaceful, calm

556)Vrishakapih - The root cause of sustaining Virtues

557)Ushna - Hot, Scorching due to swallowing poison the most sizzling 'Halahal' into His Throat

558)Grihapati - Lord of House

559)Krishna - Sacchidanand , always filled with Eternal Bliss, He who is in the form of Krishna

560)Samarth - Capable of doing everything

561)Anarthanashana - Destroyer of Evil Calamities

562)Adharmashatru - Opponent of Unrighteousness, enemy of evil

563)Ajneya - Unknowable and Unreachable

564)Puruhutah Purushthithah - Commended and devoted by multitude of devotees

565)Brahma Garbhah - He who is having

Bramha in his belly

566)Brihad Garbhah - He holds the entire Brahmanda in His abdomen

567)Dharmadhenu - Cow of Virtue

568)Dhanagama - Source of Wealth

569)Jagaddhitaishi - Well-wisher of Universe

570)Sugatah - Immersed in noble thoughts and actions

571)Kumarah - Shiva in the shape of Lord Kartikeya

572)Kushalagam - Source of Welfare

573)Hiranyavarno Jyotishman - Golden coloured and luminous

574)Nana bhutaratha - He who is with Bhutas and Piscachas

575)Dwani - Sound

576)Arag - Devoid of Attachments

577)Nayanadhyaksha - The Presider of Eyes and Eyesight

578)Viswamitra - Viswamitra the Great Sage

579)Dhaneshwar - Lord of Wealth

580)Bramhajyoti - Brilliance of Bramhan,

Light of Bramhan, Supreme Bramhan

581)Vasudhama - Shining with the lustre of gold and jewels on his body

582)Mahajyotirnuttam - Filled with Great Splendor, Excellent

583)Matamaha - Maternal Grandfather

584)Matarishva Nabhasvan - Wind God, Vaporous Air

585)Nagaharadhrk - He who is wearing garlands of Snakes

586)Pulatsya - Sage Pulatsya

587)Pulaha - Sage Pulaha

588)Agastya - Sage Agastya

589)Jatukarnya - Sage Jatukarnya

590)Parashar - Sage Parashar

591)Niravarananirvara - Uncovered and unprevented

592)Vairancya - In the form of Rudra who manifested himself through Bramha, Son of Bramha

593)Vishtarshrava - He who is in the form of Glorious Vishnu

594)Atmabhu - Self-born, Swayambu, self-illuminated

595)Aniruddha - Unobstructed, uncontrollable

596)Atri - Sage Atri

597)Jnanmurti - Knowledge personified, Knowledge bodied

598)Mahayasha - Boundless famed

599)Loka Veeragrani - The Head of the Valiant

600)Veer - Heroic, Brave

601)Chanda - Very angry with the Evil Minded

602)Satyaparakrama - Truthfully Valiant

603)Vyala Kalpa - He who is in the company of poisonous Snakes

604)Maha Kalpa - Extraordinary Capable, Time of Time

605)Kalpavriksha - He who is like a Tree of Kalpavriksha granting desires, wish-yielding Kalpa tree

606)Kaladhara - He who is possessing Arts, He who keeps moon as an ornament on his head

607)Alankrishnu - Ornamented and illuminated

608)Achal - Firm, stable and unmoving

609)Rochishnu - Radiant and Bright

610)Vikramonnathah - Lofty in Valour, Bravery of the Highest order

611)Aayu Shabdapati - Lord of Age and Speech, Regulator of Age and Ruler of Vedas

612)Vegi plavana - Instant grantor if desires

613)Sikhi saarathih - Facilitator of the tasks of Agni or Fire

614)Asansrushta - Untouched

615)Atithi - Guest

616)Shakrapramathi - Suppressor of Indra's false pride, he who destroyed Ego of Indra(King of Gods)

617)Padapasana - Tree seated, He who sits on a Tree or under a tree

618)Vasushrava - He who is full of victorious wealth

619)Havyavaha - He who is in the form of Agni (Fire)

620)Pratapta - Heated, He who is in the form

of Sun giving tremendous heat

621)Vishva Bhojana - He who shallows entire Universe at the time of Universe, Universe dieted

622)Japya - Worthy of being worshipped with Japas(Chanting)

623)Jaradhishman - Subduer of Old Age

624)Lohita Tanunapat - Red , Fire God

625)Brihadasvaha - He who is in custody of huge Horses, Owner of Huge Horses

626)Nabhoyoni - Cause of Sky

627)Supratik - He who is having attractive limbs and features, Beautiful Bodied

628)Tamishrah - He who saves devotees from dark ignorance, Destroyer of Darkness

629)Nidagasthapanah - Hot Summer

630)Megh - Cloud

631)Swasha - Beautiful eyed

632)Para Puranjayah - He who defeated Enemies like Tripurasur

633)Sukhaanila - Provider of Cool air comfort

634)Sunishpannah - Creator of this charming World

635)Surabhi Shishiratmak - Fragrant Winter Season

636)Vasantho Madhava - Spring Season

637)Greeshmah - Summer Season

638)Nabhasya - Month of Bhadrapada

639)Bhijavahan - Carrier of seeds

640)Angira Guru - Sage Angira

641)Atreya - Sage Durvasa son of Atri Rishi

642)Vimal - Figure of Purity, soft

643)Vishvavahan - Carrier of the burden of the whole World

644)Paavan - Pure, clean, holy, Sinless

645)Sumatirvidvan - Intelligent, Knowledgeable, Fair minded

646)Trividya - Source of Three Vedas Rig, Yajur, Sama Vedas

647)Varavahana - He who is having best vehicle viz ; Bull which denotes Dharma Righteousness

648)Manobuddhiahankar - Mind, Intellect,

and Ego

649)Kshetrajna - Self, soul

650)Kshetra Palak -He who is the Chief of the Kshetra, Lord of Fields, Lord of bodies, protector of the field

651)Jamadagni - Sage Jamadagni

652)Balnidhi - Storehouse of Energy

653)Vigaala - He who showers water of Ganga river from his matted hairs

654)Vishvagalava - Universal Abode

655)Aghor - Non-terrible

656)Anuttara - Unsurpassed, Best, Supreme Being

657)Yagya Shreshtha - Supreme Yagya, Supreme Sacrifice

658)Nihshreyasprada - Bestower of Salvation, Auspicious, Well-being

659)Shail - Mountain

660)Gagan kundabha - White colour bodies like moon, resembling the sky flower kunda

661)Danavari - Enemy of Asuras / Danavas (Demons)

662)Arindama - Suppressor of Enemies

663)Rajanaijanakashcharu - Beautiful, Attractive

664)Nishalya - Indisputable

665)Lokashalyadhrik - He who takes sufferings of Devotees upon himself

666)Chaturved - Originator of Four Vedas, He who is known through four Vedas

667)Chaturbhava - Bestower of Dharma (Righteousness), Artha(Economic Values), Kama(Pleasure) and Moksha (Liberation/Salvation), Shiva the Expression of the Four 'Bhavas' viz. Dharma, Artha, Kama, Moksha

668)Chaturshchaturpriya - Skillfull, Best among intellectual people, Fond of Skillful

669)Amnaya - Vedas

670)Samamnayah - He who recites Vedas very well

671)Tirthadev Shivalaya - Lord of Holy places, Supreme Deity of 'Thirthas' or the Holy Places, Shiva Temple

672)Bahurupa - Multiformed, Shiva with several names and forms

673)Maharupa - Immense-formed

674)Sarvarupa Charachar - He who

manifested himself in all forms, he who pervades mobile and immobile beings, all pervasive lord

675)Nyaya Nirmayak Nyayi - Essence of Justice, Decider of Justice, Vindicator of Justice

676)Nyayagamya - Knowable through Justice

677)Niranjan - Spotless

678)Sahastramurdha - Thousand Headed

679)Devendra - Lord of Devas

680)Sarvashastra Prabhanjana - Breaker of Weapons and Missiles of his Enemies in

Battlefield

681)Munda - Shaven headed

682)Virup - Multiformed

683)Vikrant - Most Energetic and Strong

684)Dandi - Holder of 'Kala Danda' deciding the fates of all, staff holder

685)Danta - Suppressor of mind and senses in general he who helps his Devotees to gain control over mind and senses

686)Gunottam - Filled with Good Qualities

687)Pingalaksh - Tawny Eyed

688)Janadhyaksha - The Prime force of humanity

689)Nilagriva - Blue-necked

690)Niramaya - He who is free from diseases

691)Sahastrabahu - Thousand armed

692)Sarvesh - Lord of all, Ultimate God of all

693)Sharanyah - Final Refuge for Protection

694)Sarvalokadhrk - Supporter of all the worlds

695)Padmasan - Lotus-seated, Seated in Lotus like posture with crossed legs as the right feet on left thigh and left feet on right thigh

696)Param Jyothi - Greatest Splendour, of the highest possible glitter

697)Paramparya Phalaprada - Bestower of Benefits

698)Padmagarbha - Lotus wombed , Vishnu , he who is in the form of Vishnu (Lotus originated from the belly of Vishnu)

699)Mahagarbha - Huge-wombed, his belly is storehouse of Infinite Universes

700)Vishvagarbha - He who is having Universe in his Womb

701)Vichakshan - Skillful

702)Paravarajna - Knower of Greatest and smallest, Knower of Cause and Creator

703)Varada - Bestower of Boons

704)Mahaswan - He who creates loud sound with his Damru

705)Devasurgurudev - Guru or Guide of Devas(Gods) and Asuras(Demons)

706)DevasuraNamaskrithah - He who is saluted by Devas and Asura

707)Varenya - Superior

708)Devasura Mahamitra - He who is impartial to both Devas and Asuras and is a great friend of both

709)Devasura Maheshwara - Great God of Devas and Asuras

710)Devasureshwar - Ruler of Gods and Demons, Lord of Devas and Asuras

711)Divya - Divine Being

712)Devasura Mahashraya - Refuge point of Devas and asuras

713)Devdevmay - God of Gods , Great God

714)Acintya - Inconceivable, He who is

beyond mind and thoughts

715)(a)Devatma - Soul of all Deities
(b)Atmasambhava - Self born

716)Sadyoni - Origin of Srishti (Creation)

717)Asuravyaghra - Hunter of Asuras, he who is fierce like Tiger and slayer of Demons

718)Deva Simhah - Lion among the Devas, King of Gods, Supreme among Gods

719)Divakar - Sun

720)Vibhudhagrachar Shreshtha - Supreme among Gods, Highest

721)Sarva Devottamottama - Best among Gods

722)Shivgyanrat - Totally absorbed in Awareness about himself or Shivajnana

723)Sriman - Store House of Prosperity

724)Shikhishriparvatrupa - He who is in the form of Kartikeya and fond of Shaila Parvat

725)Vajrahasta - He who is in the form of Indra holding Vajra (Thunderbolt) in his Hands

726)Siddhakadga - He who is possessing a sword and uses it to kill his Enemies in Battlefield without fail

727)Narasimha Nipatahanah - He who incarnated as Sharbha and defeated Narasimha Incarnation of Vishnu

728)Bramhachari - Celibate, traverser of the path of Bramhan

729)Lokachari - He who analyses the happenings of various Lokas

730)Dharmachari - Performer of Virtuous deeds always

731)Dhanadhip - Lord of Wealth

732)Nandi - He who is in the form of Nandi (Attendant of Shiva)

733)Nandishwara - Identical with Nandishwara

734)Anant - Infinite

735)Nagnavratadhara - He who uses directions as his clothes, he who is not wearing clothes, Naked

736)Suchi - Always Pure

737)Lingadhyaksha - Presiding Deity of Shivalinga (Sign of Shiva which is worshipped)

738)Suradhyaksha - Presiding Chief of Devas

739)Yogadhyaksha - Presiding Deity of Yoga

Practioner, Lord of Yoga, Yogeshwar

740)Yugavaha - He who rotates cycle of Yugas

741)Swadharma - He who is absorbed in his own act of Srishti or Creation

742)Swargata - He who resides in Swarga (Heaven)

743)Swargswar - He who is Glorified in Heaven

744)SwaramayaSwana - Originator of sonorous sounds of Swaras, he whose sound consist of 7 Swaras

745)Banadhyaksha - Controller of Banasura Demon, Supervisor of Arrows

746)Bhijakarta - Creator of Seeds

747)Dharmakhrudharmasambhav - Creator of Dharma(Righteous Conduct), Follower of Dharma(Righteousness)

748)Dambh - Illusionary, he who examines the genuineness of devotees by various forms and acts

749)Alobha - He who has no greed

750)Arthavicchambhu - Auspicious Shiva who is knower of everyone's thought

751)Sarvabhutmaheshwar - Great God of all Living Beings

752)Smashananilaya - Dweller in Cremation Ground

753)Tryaksha - Three Eyed

754)Setu - Bridge

755)Apratimakruti - Beautiful Bodied, Unequalled Featured

756)Lokotthara sphutaloka - Most Excellent and Radiant in the World

757)Tryambaka - Three eyed

758)Nagbhushan - He who uses Serpents as his Ornaments

759)Andhakari - Killer of Andhakasura Demon

760)Makhadweshi - Demolisher of Daksha Prajapati's Yagna

761)Vishnukandharapatana - Slasher of Vishnu's head

762)Hinadosh - Devoid of Faults and Impurities

763)Akshaygun - Epitome of endless qualities of high merit

764)Dakshari - Enemy of Daksha, Antagonist of Daksha

765)Pushadantabhita - He who broke Teeths of Pusha

766)Dhurjati - Matted haired

767)Khandaparshu - He who is having broken Axe

768)Sakalo Nishkala - Formed and Formless, with a form and without a form

769)Anagh - Devoid of Sins

770)Akaal - He who is Untouched by effect of Time

771)Sakaladhaar - Everyone's Support

772)Pandhurabha - He whose body colour is white

773)Mridonata - Blissful cosmic dancer

774)Purn - All pervasive Parabrahman Paramatma, Supreme Bramhan, Supreme God

775)Purayita - He who fulfills wishes of his Devotees

776)Punya - Sacred, holiest , purest of all

777)Sukumar - Very tender and delight, Kumar Kartikeya

778)Sulochana - Attractive and good eyed

779)Samageyapriya - Lover of Samaveda recital

780)Akrur - Merciful

781)Punyakirti - Meritorious famed, Famous owing to Great Merit and Virtue

782)Anamaya - Devoid of Diseases, free from sickness

783)Manojava - As fast as mind, he who is having speed of mind, quick in solving problems of devotees

784)Tirthkara - Creator of Holy places,

maker of Holy Centres

785)Jatila - Matted Haired

786)Jiviteshwar - Giver of Life to all

787)Jeevitantakara - Cause of End of Life, he who gives Life and takes it away

788)Nitya - Eternal

789)Vasureta - Golden semened

790)Vasuprada - Giver of Wealth, Bestower of Riches

791)Sadgati - Goal of the Good, Ultimate goal, Conducter of Noble path

792)Satkriti - Performer of Merits and Virtues

793)Siddhi - He who grants fruitful results to dedicated endeavours

794)Sajjati - He who awards good births to those who are noble and devoted, Creator of Noble souls

795)Khalakantak - Destroyer of Evil

796)Kaladhara - Possesser of Arts , Bestower of Arts

797)Mahakaalbhuta - Time of Time, Creator of Time, Mahakaal Jyotirlinga

798)Satayaparana - Devoted to Truth, He who inspires Truthfulness among all human beings and is the final refuge to them

799)Lokalavanyakarta - Creator of Beauty of Worlds

800)Lokottarasukhalaya - Abode of Eternal everlasting Happiness of the worlds

801)(a)Chandrasanjivan - He who is in the form of Somanath , he who recovered life of Chandra Moon God (b)Sastha - Law maker and Punishes the Evil Forces

802)Lokaguddha - He who is present everywhere in the world yet unknown

803)Mahadhipah - Great God , Maheshwar, Maha Ishwar, Highest Level of Superiority over the World

804)Lokabandhu Lokanath - Protector of the Worlds, He who treats all the Beings of the World as his own relatives

805)Krtajna - Grateful

805)Krtajna - Grateful

806)Kirti Bhushana - Adorned with Reputation

807)Anapayokshara - Imperishable and inexhaustible

808)Kanta - Brilliant

809)Sarvashastrabhrtavara - Foremost among bearers of weapons

810)Tejomaya Dhyutidhara - Full of Brilliance, Radiance and resplendence

811)Lokanamagrani - World's best, Honour of World, God of Everyone

812)Anu - Subtle, he who is present in the tiniest atom

813)Suchismitha - He who has a charming and petty smile

814)Prassanatma - Always happy soul

815)Durjey - Unconquerable and bound only for Devotion and complete surrender

816)Durathikrama - Unsurpassable

817)Jyotirmaya - Full of Extraordinary Luminosity

818)Jagannatha - Lord of Worlds, the Unique Lord of Cosmos

819)Nirakar - Formless, He who has neither shape nor form, formless aspect of Shiva which is Eternal and Everlasting

820)Jaleshwar - God of Water, God of Water bodies

821)Thumbaveen - The Greatest Expert of Music in playing Musical Instrument Veena made of gourd

822)Mahakopah - Angriest and the most ferocious while engaged in activities of destruction

823)Vishok - Devoid of Sorrows

824)Shoknashan - Destroyer of Sorrows

825)Trilokapa - Lord of Theee Worlds, Chief Administrator of the Three Lokas

826)Trilokesha - God of Three Worlds

827)Sarvashuddhi - Purifier of all the Beings

828)Adhoshaja - He who is beyond Mind and senses

829)Avyakta Lakshana Deva - He whose features are unknown

830)Vyaktaavyakta - Manifest and unmanifest

831)Vishampati - Lord of Subjects

832)Varshil - He whose behaviour is best

833)Vara Gunah - Ornamented with Excellent Gunas(Qualities) or attributes

834)Saar - Essence

835)Maandhan - He who considers high merit as wealth

836)Maya मय - Embodiment of Happiness

837)Bramha - Creator of Universe, Shiva who manifested as Bramha

838)Vishnu Prajapala - He who manifested as Vishnu preserver of this Universe, Protector of Subjects

839)Hamsa - Swan

840)Hamsa Gati - Liberator as the traverser of Hamsa or Swan guiding Yogis

841)Vaya - Bird, Eagle Bird

842)(a)Vedha Vidhata Dhata - He who manifested as Gods like Bramha, Dhata and Vidhata (b)Vedha - Famed name of Shiva as Creator (c)Vidhata - Disposer of Fate, decider of Fate of each being (d)Dhata - Sustainer

843)Shrashta - Creator of Universe

844)Harta - Destroyer

845)Chaturmukha - He who manifested as Four Headed Bramha

846)Kailashshikharavasi - Resident on top of Kailash Mountain

847)Sarvavasi - All pervasive, He who resides in all, He who resides as the 'Antaratma' or the

Inner Soul of every Being

848)Sadagati - Unstoppable, Always moving

849)Hiranyagarbha - Bramha

850)Druhina - Bramha

851)Bhutapala - Protector of all Living Beings

852)Bhupati - Lord of the Earth

853)Sadyogi - Best Yogi , Best Spiritual Practioner

854)Yog Vidyogi - Learned Guide to Yogis, Yogi who is knower of Yoga

855)Varad - Bestower of Boons

856)Bramhan Priya - Fond of Bramhins, Affectionate to Brahmanas

857)Devapriya Devanatha - Fond of Gods, Interested in the well being of Devas, Chief of Deva ganas

858)Devajna - He who encourages Devas to acquire higher knowledge

859)Devchintak - He who thinks about the Welfare of Devatas, He who is always engrossed in the welfare of Devas and also to those who pray to Devas

860)Vishamaaksha - He who is having

Poisonous Fire in his Third Eye

861)Visalaksha - He who has broad and attractive Eyes, big eyed

862)Vrishado Vrishvardhan - Bestower of Righteousness

863)Nirmama - Detached

864)Nirahankar - Free from Ego

865)Nirmoha - Free from Delusion

866)Nirupadrav - Harmless

867)Darpaha Darpada - He who subdues the

Arrogant

868)Drpta - Proud

869)Sarvarthaparivartaka - Cause of change in everything

870)Sahasrajit - Victorious after slaying thousands of enemies

871)Sahastrarchi - He who is having countless rays of radiance

872)Snigdha Prakriti Dakshinah - Merciful, Compassionate, soft, very talented and soft-minded owing to natural amicability

873)Bhuta Bhavya Bhavannath - Lord of Past,

Present and Future

874)Prabhava - Cause of Creation

875)Bhutinashan - He who wipes out the wealth of Enemies, Destroyer of prosperity of wicked

876)Artha - He who encourages the Wealth earned by hard work

877)Anartha - He knocks down money earned by foul means

878)Mahakosh - Great Treasure, Storehouse of Wealth

879)Parakarayaika Pandit - Sole Scholar in

other's Activities

880)Nishkantakah - He who is devoid of hurdles viz. Kama, Krodha, Lobha, Moha, Mada, Matsara

881)Krithanand - He who has uninterrupted happiness

882)Nirvyaja Vyajamardana - Free from false pretexts, Suppressor of False Pretexts

883)Satvavaan - He who possesses Satwa Qualities, Mode of Goodness

884)Satvik - Essentially of Satva Guna, Devoted to Satva Nature (Mode of Goodness)

885)Satyakirti - He who has truthful glory

886)Sneha Krithagama - Being friendly and affectionate, He exhorts the Essence of Sciptures to devotees, Affectionate one who gives Knowledge of Agamas for welfare and well-being

887)Akampita - Non trembling, unaffected

888)Gunagrahi - He who has respect for Good Qualities of his Devotees, Grasping Goodness, He who gracefully accepts even small offerings from devotees

889)Naikatma Naikakarmakrith - He who is Multiple souled and performs multiple actions

890)Suprit - He who is full of Great Happiness

891)Sumukh - Beautiful Faced

892)Suksma - Subtle , of Tiny Form; but capable of expanding endlessly; 'Sarva gathah Sookshmam'

893)Sukar - He who is having Beautiful hands, of good hands

894)Dakshinanila - He who is in the form of pleasant winds from Southern side

895)Nandiskandadhaar - He who comfortably sits on Nandi

896)Dhurya - Worthy of being considered on Head, Capable of completing his work, He holds innumerable Beings of Creation

897)Prakat - He who appears in front of his Devotees to bless them

898)Pritivardhan - He who enriches the love of devotees, Enhancer of Love

899)Aparajit - Undefeatable, Unconquerable

900)Sarvasatva - Completely in mode of Goodness

901)Govinda - He who gives place to Devotees in Goloka

902)Satvavahan - He who makes bull as his Vehicle (Bull is embodiment of Righteousness and Goodness)

903)Adhrta - He who does not needs anyone Support , Devoid of any Support

904)Svadhrta - Self Supported

905)Siddha   -   Spiritually   Developed, possessing spiritual powers

906)Putamurti - Pure Figure

907)Yashodhan - Wealth of Great Reputation, Storehouse of Success

908)Varaha Shringa Dhrkchhrungi - He who

is holding horn of Boar Incarnation of Vishnu viz; Varaha

909)Balwan - Powerful, Strong

910)Akanayaka - One Leader of all, Singular and Ultimate

911)Shrutiprakash - Illuminator of Vedas, Giver of Vedas

912)Shrutiman - He who has complete Knowledge of Vedas, He is in the possession of Vedas always

913)Ekabandhu - He who is Ultimate Support of all (He alone is permanent and worldly relations are temporary. He is

Ultimate Goal of all. Relation of Jeeva is permanent with Paramatma Shiv)

914)Anekakruta - He who creates Entire Universe in different ways, He who is Single Entity but creates a multitude

915)Sri Vatsala Shivarambha - He who is initiator of propitiousness to Vishnu and Lakshmi, He who is Auspicious for Vishnu

916)Shantabhadra - Peaceful and Embodiment of Auspiciousness

917)Sama - Impartial

918)Yash - Fame, Embodiment of Success and Fame

919)Bhushan - He who rests on Earth, He who is laying on Ground

920)Bhushan - Ornamented , Bestower of Wealth to all deserving

921)Bhuti - Auspicious, He who is the well wisher to one and all

922)Bhoota Krit - He who is the Generator of All

923)Bhutabhavana - Conceiver of all Living Beings

924)Akampa - Non trembling

925)Bhaktikaya - Embodiment of Devotion

926)Kaalha - Destroyer of Kala, Mahakal who spares none during the time of destruction

927)Nilalohitha - Retainer of poisonous flames by which his throat turned blue

928)Satyavrat Mahatyagi - Unique Practitioner of Truthfulness and Greatest Renunciator

929)Nitya Shanti Parayana - Eternal Observer of Peace

930)Paearthavrtti Varada - Actively engaged in welfare of others

931)Virakta - Unattached, Celibate

932)Visharada - Skillfull

933)Shubhada Shubhakarta - Bestower of Auspiciousness and maker of auspicious circumstances

934)Shubhanama Shubhaswayam - Auspicious formed , auspicious named

935)Anarthita - He who grants wishes without asking for them

936)Aguna - Devoid of Attributes and features, Attribute less form of Shiva

937)Saakshi Akartha - He who is the Evidence of Creation executed by Maya or Illusion

938)Kanakaprabha - Illuminated, Radiant and Lustrous like Gold

939)Svabhavabhadra - Naturally Good

940)Madhyastha - Stationed in the Middle

941)Satrughna - Destroyer of Enemies

942)Vighnanashan - Destroyer of obstacles

943)Shikhandi Kavachi Shuli - (a)Shikhandi - He who is wearing peacock feather on his Head (b)Kavachi - He who is wearing a shield (c)Shuli - Holding spear in his hands

944)Jati Mundi cha Kundali - He who is matted haired and also he who is having clean shaven head , he who is wearing ear rings

945)Amrityu - Deathless, He who has no Demise because he has no Beginning or End

946)Sarvadrk Simha - Best among Knowledgeable people

947)Tejorashi Mahamahi - Storehouse of Light, Great Splendour, Great Jewel

948)Asankheyo Prameyatma - He who has countless Forms, Unique and indestructible Super Soul

949)Viravan Virya Kovidah - Master of Bravery and Might

950)Vedyah - He whom Yogis seek to learn all about

951)Viyogatma - He who lived as a Celibate and detached soul when he got separated from his wife Sati

952)Paaravaar Muniswarah - He who knows all about past, present, future and he who is Great Sage, He who is Supreme Sage whom Humanity and Devas yearn to know all about

953)Anuttamo Duradharsh - Most Excellent , Supreme and incapable of being attacked, Unconquerable

954)Madhura Priya Darshana - Unimaginably stunning and attractive figured

955)Suresh - Lord of Gods

956)Sharanam - Ultimate Refuge

957)Sarva - Destroyer

958)Shabda Bramha Sataam Gatih - He who is in the form of Pranava Omkara, he who is Ultimate refuge for Sadhus and the Virtuous

959)Kalapaksha - He who uses Kala (Time) for the task of Creation, Maintenance and Destruction

960)Kalakala - Destroyer of Death, Superior to Time

961)Kankanikrtavasuki - He who uses Vasuki

snake as a Wristlet in his hands

962)Maheshwas - Great Archer

963)Mahibharta - Lord of Earth, Supporter of Earth

964)Nishkalanka - Stainless, Blemishless

965)Visrunkhala - He who bestows the power of breaking chains of Maya or Illusion

966)Dyumanirstharani - He assumes the form of Surya (Jewel in the Sky) and shines, he who helps his Devotees to swim across the Ocean of 'Samsara' or Maya

967)Dhanyah - He who blesses those who do

service to humanity

968)Siddhida Siddhisadhana - Giver of Siddhis (Spiritual powers), He enables in guiding those who seek attainment of Siddhis, Spiritual Practitioner

969)Viswatha Sanvrta - He who is Present all over the Universe through his Maya

970)Stutya - Worthy of Glorification

971)Vyudhoraskah - Broad chested

972)Mahabhujah - Broad shouldered, he who is having Great Arms

973)Sarvayoni - Source of Everything

974)Niratanka - Free from Terror

975)Nara Narayana Priyah - He who is very dear to two Sages Nara and Narayana, He who was extremely pleased with the Twin Sages Nara and Narayana

976)Nirlepah Nishprapanchatma - Uncontaminated, Super Soul without the Worldly features of Panchabhutas

977)Nirvyangya - Creator of Special Physical parts

978)Vyanga Naasanah - Destroyer of distorted Body Parts, Destroyer of Mutilated state

979)Sravya - Worthy of Praise, Glorification, appreciation, respect and Worship

980)Stavapriya - Fond of praise

981)Stota - He who praises his Devotees for their Devotion and Hardwork

982)Vyasmurti - Shiva in the Form of Veda Vyasa

983)Niramkusha - Fully Independent

984) Nirvadhyamayopaya - Blemishless Formed

985)Vidyarashi - Storehouse of Knowledge

986)Rasa Priyah - He who is fond of Nectar of Eternal Bliss of Bramhan (Upanishads declare Bhagwan Shiva as Bramhan. Shiva is always Immersed in that Highest State of Bramhan. He is Drinking Nectar of Eternal Bliss. He meditates on his own form)

987)Prashant Buddhi - Cool minded, He who has calm Intellect

988)Ashunna - Unbeaten

989)Samgrahi - Collecter, He who collects Good Devotees

990)Nityasundar - Always Beautiful

991)Vaiyaghra Dhurya - He who has Tigerish

Nature and considered as the Head

992)Dhatrish - Lord of Earth

993)Shakalya - Sage Shakalya

994)Sharvaripati - Lord of Night

995)Paramarthaguru Datta Suri - Wise and Real Preceptor Datta (Guru Dattatreya) , He who is in the form of Datta Guru

996)Aashrita Vatsala - He who is fond of his Devotees (Devotees consider Shiva as their Ultimate Refuge, Shiva as Shelter. Shiva is fond of such Devotees)

997)Soma - He who is allied with his Consort

Uma (Soma = Shiva + Uma)

998)Rasajna - Knower of Nectar of Devotion

999)Rasad - Bestower of Sweetnees, Giver of Nectar of Love

1000)Sarva Satvavanambanah - Supreme Supporter of All, Supreme Power, Supporter of all Living Beings

Natraja the God of Dance
(Nityanritya - He who does Tandava dance daily, He who is eternally doing cosmic Tandava dance)

Chapter 5
About Greatness of Bhagwan Shiva and his Name

"VidyAsu SrutirutkrishTA rudraikAdaSini Srutau | tatra panchaksharl tasyAm Siva ityakshara dvayam ||" (Karana Agama Chapter 8 Verse 4)

"Among all sources of knowledge (vidyas), the Vedas are supreme. In the Vedas, Sri Rudram is supreme. In the Rudram, the Panchakshari mantra (namah SivAya) is supreme and in Panchakshari mantra itself, the two syllables 'Siva' is supreme!"

So, Knowledge of Shrutis is Best (Sarvottama). Vedas are highest source of Knowledge. Shrutis are Vedas and Upanishads which are highest of all Studies. Therefore, Shrutis are given more importance than Smritis.

In the Vedas, Sri Rudram is Supreme. Sri Rudram is a Hymn dedicated to Lord Shiva. It is present in Taittiriya Samhita of Yajurveda. There is no other Hymn which is Superior to Rudram.

In Sri Rudram, Panchakshari Mantra (Namah Shivaya) is Supreme.

In Panchakshari Mantra, the two syllables 'Siva' is supreme!" Therefore, Shiva is the essence of Vedas. By reciting the "Shiva Shiva" all the sins are vanished. Shiva is ready to give Post of Bramha and Vishnu to the one who is chanting the name of Shiva with utmost devotion.

1)Supreme Shastras - Shrutis (Vedas and Upanishads)

2)Supreme Hymn - Sri Rudram present in Taittiriya Samhita of Yajurveda

3)Supreme Mantra - Panchakshari Mantra (Namah Shivaya)

4)Supreme Syllables - "Siva"

5)Supreme God - Shiva

Thank You